# JAMES MONROE

The Era of Good Feelings

Written by Julie Lorang
In collaboration with Thomas Jacquemin
Translated by Rebecca Neal

History 50MINUTES.com

# JAMES MONROE

## KEY INFORMATION

- **Born:** 28 April 1758 in Westmoreland County, Virginia.
- **Died:** 4 July 1831 in New York.
- **Election dates:**
    - 4 December 1816
    - 6 December 1820.
- **Length of presidency:** eight years.
- **Main achievements:**
    - the Missouri Compromise (1820)
    - the Monroe Doctrine (1823).

## INTRODUCTION

James Monroe was the fifth President of the United States of America. He had two consecutive terms in the White House, between 1817 and 1825. Having been ambassador, Senator and Secretary of State before attaining the highest office in the country, Monroe became known above all for his diplomatic talents, as well as the Missouri Compromise and the doctrine that bears his name.

The period spanning his two terms has been described as the "Era of Good Feelings" due to the relative political unity and prosperity that followed the two wars between the USA and Great Britain (the American War of Independence, also known as the American Revolutionary War, from 1775 to 1783, and the War of 1812 from 1812 to 1815). The president made the most of this favourable context to expand

American territory towards the south and the west. The implementation of the Monroe Doctrine, which continues to govern American foreign policy even today, gave the country a leading place on the international political stage during the late 18th and early 19th centuries.

On the national level, however, the president had to deal with fierce tensions between the abolitionist North and the slaveholding South. He managed to soothe these tensions for a few years thanks to the Missouri Compromise. Nonetheless, political and ethical divisions resurfaced at the end of his term and would eventually lead to the American Civil War (1861-1865).

# BIOGRAPHY

Portrait of James Monroe.

# A HEROIC YOUTH

James Monroe was born on 28 April 1758 to a family of wealthy farmers in Westmoreland County, Virginia. The early years of the future president were marked by the premature deaths of his parents: his mother Elizabeth Jones (1730-1774) died before he reached adulthood, and his father Spence Monroe (1727-1774) died shortly afterwards. The orphaned boy was then taken in by his uncle Joseph Jones (1727-1805), who sent him to study at the College of William and Mary in Williamsburg, Virginia.

Monroe's studies were interrupted by the outbreak of the American Revolution in April 1775. Like many students in Virginia, he decided to join the Continental Army and fight for his country's independence.

During the war, Monroe distinguished himself through his bravery and took part in several major battles. In particular, he fought on the front lines during the Battle of Trenton (26 December 1776), where he sustained an injury to his left shoulder. Thanks to his courage and loyalty, he was quickly promoted to the rank of captain.

During this revolutionary period, Monroe also made several important connections: he fought alongside George Washington (American general and statesman, 1732-1799), who would become the first President of the United States, and met Thomas Jefferson (American statesman, 1743-1826), then Governor of Virginia and later the third President of the United States. Jefferson quickly became Monroe's close friend and political mentor.

## EARLY POLITICAL CAREER IN VIRGINIA AND EUROPE

After the war, Monroe studied law and embarked on a political career which began in his home state. In 1782, he was elected to the Virginia House of Delegates and represented his state at the Congress of the Confederation, which governed the United States between 1781 and 1789. His precise and thoughtful work allowed him to stand out once again, and he became a Senator in 1790.

During his term, Monroe joined forces with two other Virginian politicians – his friend, Thomas Jefferson, and James Madison (future President of the United States, 1751-1836) – to establish the Democratic-Republican Party.

Also at this time, he married Elizabeth Kortright (1768-1830), the daughter of a New York merchant, with whom he would have two daughters, as well as a son who died in childhood.

Portrait of Elizabeth Monroe.

From 1794 onwards, Monroe's career took him to Europe, where he served as Minister Plenipotentiary (meaning ambassador) in Paris and London. This diplomatic post allowed him to spend time in France during the Revolution (1789-1799) and the Empire of Napoleon Bonaparte (1769-1821), and in Britain under the rule of King George III (King of Great Britain and Ireland, 1738-1820), thus giving him the opportunity to perfect his knowledge of Europe and international affairs.

He also distinguished himself in Europe through his key role in the negotiations that led to the purchase of Louisiana from France in 1803. The acquisition of this vast territory, which was far larger than present-day Louisiana, allowed the USA to double its area.

## FROM SECRETARY OF STATE TO PRESIDENT

When the Democratic-Republican James Madison was elected president in 1811, he made Monroe his right-hand man by appointing him Secretary of State. One year later, tensions between Britain and America were running so high following the independence of the USA that a war broke out. Madison once again chose Monroe to fill an essential post in these troubled times, namely Secretary of War. This double nomination was a decisive moment in his political career because it allowed him to demonstrate the breadth of his diplomatic and military knowledge. It was also remarkable because, even to this day, it remains the only time this has happened in the history of America.

At the end of the war, Monroe ran in the presidential elections and defeated his Federalist opponent Rufus King (1755-1827) in a landslide, winning 84% of the votes. On 4 March 1817, he was sworn in as the fifth President of the United States. His presidency is known as the "Era of Good Feelings" due to the political consensus and the lack of op-position to the Democratic-Republicans, who were virtually the only party in the country. Monroe himself had very few opponents, to the point that he did not need to campaign to be reelected.

During his presidency, Monroe drove American foreign policy forward by delivering his famous doctrine and temporarily resolving the question of slavery thanks to the Missouri Compromise.

Monroe retired from political life after his second term and returned to live in his native Virginia. After the death of his wife in 1830, he moved to New York, where he died in 1831, on 4 July, American Independence Day.

# POLITICAL, SOCIAL AND ECONOMIC CONTEXT

James Monroe lived through and took part in many of the major events of early American history, including the War of Independence and the birth of the new country and its institutions. His presidency should therefore be understood as part of a very specific context: that of a young country in search of its identity.

## THE BIRTH OF THE UNITED STATES OF AMERICA

### American independence

Monroe is the last president to have fought for his country's independence. The American War of Independence took place between 1775 and 1783 and pitted the 13 colonies of North America against Great Britain, which was at that time a great colonial power. The main reason for the uprising was the discontent of the population in the colonies, who shouldered a heavy tax burden and were not represented at the Parliament in London. France, the perennial enemy of its British neighbour, also took part in the conflict by supporting the American rebels. In this way, the Marquis de Lafayette (French politician, 1757-1834) participated in the events with the hope of putting the ideals of the Enlightenment, whose watchwords were individual free-dom and equality, into practice. Lafayette, who also played an important role in the French Revolution in 1789, hope that this country could become the world's first democracy.

While France was initially content to supply equipment to the continental troops, it officially entered the conflict in 1778.

*Washington and Lafayette at Valley Forge*, painting by John Ward Dunsmore.

The independence of the United States was officially proclaimed on 4 July 1776 by the American Congress and resulted in a confederation, within which every state retained its freedom. It also allowed the country to sever ties with the British colonists, who were driven from American territory. Thus, the United States of America was born. However, the country was still far from having found its identity.

## International relations

The new country's relationships with the European powers fluctuated depending on changes in European politics. After moving closer to revolutionary France due to their shared philosophy, the USA preferred to keep its distance following the coup d'état by Napoleon Bonaparte (French emperor, 1769-1821) in 1799. By proclaiming himself First Consul, Napoleon broke with the Republican ideal.

Shortly afterwards, Monroe's diplomatic work in France before his presidency allowed the United States to acquire the vast territory of Louisiana, which was purchased from Napoleon in 1803. French Louisiana was far larger than modern-day Louisiana, and comprised the states of Arkansas, Oklahoma, Kansas, Nebraska, Iowa, North Dakota, South Dakota, Louisiana, Colorado, Wyoming, Montana and Minnesota. This acquisition allowed the country to double its area and begin its expansion towards the west.

Relations with Great Britain remained tense in the years following the Declaration of Independence. The former coloniser found it hard to accept that the Americans favoured France for trade and decided to block European ports to American ships. This decision led to the War of 1812, which once again ended in victory for the Americans, strengthening the nascent national feeling. After its defeat, Britain abandoned its ambitions in the USA.

By the start of Monroe's presidency, the USA had managed to expand towards the south and the west and to drive the British and French colonists from its territory. However, there were still many issues at stake. In the South, there was still the European enclave of Florida, which belonged to the Spanish Crown. The American government feared that this colonial presence on their territory would be a threat to the country's independence and sovereignty.

Another significant challenge also awaited them: finding and asserting their place on the international political stage.

## AN ECONOMY BASED ON SLAVERY

A crucial question hung over the founding and emergence of the United States: the issue of slavery. The debate around a servile labour force divided the country and hindered the development of national unity.

In 1793, Eli Whitney (American inventor and industrialist, 1765-1825) invented the cotton gin, which allowed the seeds and fibre of cotton to be separated, in the South of the USA. Thanks to this new machine, cotton spinning became mechanised and the price of this valuable fibre decreased. Consequently, the economic development of the Southern states was based on growing cotton, and these states found trading partners in Europe, thanks in particular to British factories which purchased raw materials from the USA. As such, the cotton trade gradually superseded the tobacco trade and became the main source of wealth in the Southern states of the country. However, cultivating this crop required a sizeable workforce, and the Southern planters were quick to acquire African-born slaves. This servile and exploited workforce allowed landowners to increase their production at a lower cost. However, a disadvantage of cotton growing was that it quickly exhausted the soils, which means that the planters regularly needed to move to new land.



In this way, the Southern states established an economy based on slavery and imported black populations en masse into their country. The development of the North, whose economy was mainly based on industry, was very different. As its industry did not require a servile labour force, it was opposed to slavery, which it saw as contrary to the country's democratic ideals.

When America gained its independence, the black American population was estimated at 750 000 individuals, 90% of whom lived in the South. While slavery remained firmly rooted in that part of the country, it gradually disappeared from the centre and the North: Massachusetts abolished it in 1783, and New York freed its slaves between 1785 and 1799.

However, the United States Constitution of 1776, based on the Enlightenment philosophy which proclaimed individual freedom and equality between individuals, avoided the question of slavery and in this way tacitly condoned it. In spite of the abolitionist ideas of the first presidents, the particular economic situation of the Southern states complicated the debate. In the early 19th century, a fragile balance was preserved between supporters of slavery and abolitionists thanks to the fact that there were equal numbers of free and slave states, and they enjoyed the same representation in the Senate. When a new territory, Missouri, wanted to join the country as a slave state, this balance was upset and tensions once again mounted between the North and South.

## THE ERA OF GOOD FEELINGS

On the political level, this lively period was, paradoxically, characterised by a calm and a unity that are rare in American history.

The first decades of the young country were nonetheless marked by the rivalry between the Democratic-Republican Party of Thomas Jefferson, James Madison and James Monroe and the Federalist Party, whose figurehead was the first American President George Washington.

The two parties differed primarily in their contrasting vision of the powers that the central government should have:

- The Democratic-Republicans relied on the states to guarantee freedoms.

- The Federalists were in favour of a strong federal state to maintain the factions. The first leaders of the Federalist Party were John Adams (1735-1826) and Alexander Hamilton (1755-1804).

They also adopted different positions with regard to the great European powers of the time, namely France and Great Britain. The Federalists admired and supported King George III (1738-1820), while the Democratic-Republicans opposed the British monarchy and supported the French Republic until Napoleon Bonaparte came to power in 1804. When the War of 1812 broke out and James Madison and James Monroe took joint action to resolve the conflict, the Federalist Party quickly lost ground and ended up definitively disappearing. Monroe's victory in the election of 1816 clearly illustrates this phenomenon: 183 votes went to the Democratic-Republican Party, compared with 34 to the Federalist candidate Rufus King. This tendency became even more pronounced in the 1820 election, when Monroe received every vote but one without even having to campaign.

### GOOD TO KNOW

Monroe's Democratic-Republican Party split into two separate parties in 1824 due to internal disagreement over the choice of a candidate for the next presidential elections. This split gave rise to the two parties that we know today: the Republicans and the Democrats. The Republican Party, represented by an elephant and the colour red, is conservative: at that time, it generally supported free trade between the states, gave an important place to religion, and claimed to be ardently opposed to slavery. Notable members of the party include Abraham Lincoln (1809-1865), who abolished slavery, Theodore Roosevelt (1858-1919), Richard Nixon (1913-1994), Ronald Reagan (1911-2004) and, more recently, George W. Bush (born in 1946).

The Democratic Party is symbolised by a donkey and the colour blue. It is a more progressive, centre-left party. Democrats are more concerned with tempering capitalism through social programmes, and defend the rights of minorities. Harry S. Truman (1884-1972), John F. Kennedy (1917-1963), Bill Clinton (born in 1946) and Barack Obama (born in 1961) were all Democratic presidents.

# HIGHLIGHTS

Three important events took place during Monroe's presidency:

- the First Seminole War followed by the Florida Purchase
- the Missouri Compromise
- the Monroe Doctrine.

These episodes allow us to better understand the domestic and foreign policy of the fifth President of the United States.

## THE FIRST SEMINOLE WAR AND THE FLORIDA PURCHASE

During his first term, Monroe found himself facing a challenging situation in the south-east of the country. While American territory was constantly expanding to the south and west, Florida remained a Spanish enclave. Since they had successfully driven out the French and English colonists, the Americans had been focusing their attentions on this last European colony, fearing that the Spanish bastion could be used a base for the Western powers to invade. The Americans also wanted to expand into Florida in order to use its rivers to develop their trade.

When Monroe came to power in 1817, there were several incidents on the border between the United States and the Spanish enclave:

- The Seminoles, a Native American tribe which occupied

part of Florida, made regular incursions into American territory and attacked farms in Georgia. According to the Americans, the Seminoles were armed and encouraged by Britain. However, they could not retaliate directly, because the tribe constantly took refuge behind the Spanish border.
- At the same time, black slaves fled the cotton fields in the South of the United States to take refuge in the Spanish enclave. The white landowners feared that their slaves would take inspiration from this situation and flee en masse towards Florida.

The American authorities were very unhappy with this situation, because they could not take direct action on Spanish territory without risking triggering a conflict with Madrid. As a former diplomat, Monroe was therefore very cautious and asked Spain to resolve the situation as soon as possible. However, he was caught unprepared when General Andrew Jackson (American statesman, 1767-1845), the commander of the American forces, decided to intervene immediately. Without asking for approval from the government, Jackson did not hesitate to hunt down Seminoles and fugitive slaves on Spanish soil. Once in Florida, the general made the most of his position to attack the Spanish forts and gain a foothold there.

American Marines search for Native Americans during the Seminole War.

This put the president in a difficult position: Jackson's actions undermined his authority, and a diplomatic crisis broke out between Washington and Madrid. However, the Secretary of State John Quincy Adams (1767-1848) observed that Jackson's actions put America in a better position than it might appear. Indeed, the Spanish were unable to respond. They did not have the necessary military capacities in North America and were preoccupied with other problems in the Caribbean and South America. Spain was effectively powerless and ended up selling Florida to the United States for just $5 million. The Adams-Onís Treaty, which ceded Florida to the United States, was signed in Washington on 22 February 1819. This agreement stipulated that the part to the east of the Mississippi River, including part of Texas, Louisiana and Florida, became American. In return, the

Americans promised to have no designs on the territory to the west and south of this border.

Some historians have used this key episode of Monroe's first term to portray him as weak and to criticise his lack of charisma and action. These historians claim that the president was unable to manage the First Seminole War and the Florida Purchase, and that the successful outcome of the episode can be attributed to Jackson and Adams alone. While it is true that Monroe did not play a major role in this acquisition, it is important to remember that he was a prudent diplomat and that he had managed to acquire Louisiana from France several years earlier thanks to his negotiating skills.

## THE MISSOURI COMPROMISE

The question of slavery was one of the main issues in American history prior to the American Civil War. Monroe's presidency was no exception to this rule, and he had to deal with ever-increasing tensions between the free states in the North and the slave states in the South following Missouri's request to join the United States.

The country had expanded constantly since its indepen-dence. The newly conquered territories were then organised into states, which had to clearly identify themselves as free or slave states. In order to preserve some degree of unity and prevent the country from collapsing, Congress decreed that the two entities should always be in balance. This precarious equilibrium was establishing by having the same number of abolitionist and slaveholding states, so that both sides had the same number of Senators (two per state). As such, Ohio (1802), Indiana (1816) and Illinois (1818) successively entered the Union and joined the free states in the North, while Louisiana (1812), Mississippi (1817) and Alabama (1819) became slave states.

In 1818, Missouri, a territory belonging to the former French Louisiana, was preparing to become the 24th state of the USA. It requested the right to practice slavery, even though it was in the North. The Northern representatives, who wanted to abolish this undemocratic practice, looked unfavourably on this request and feared that the balance of the country would shift in favour of the slave states. Heated debates in the Senate and House of Representatives ensued, until Henry Clay (1777-1852), a Senator from Kentucky, suggested a compromise that was met with widespread approval. It was finalised on 2 March 1820, and earned Clay the nickname The Great Compromiser. The arrangement was accepted by both legislative chambers on 5 March 1820 and signed into law by President Monroe the following day.

The compromise offered a resolution to the question of Missouri's membership by adding two complementary propositions:

- Missouri could enter the Union as a slave state if another free state also joined in order to maintain the balance. Consequently, Clay suggested separating Maine from Massachusetts.
- In order to stop a similarly delicate situation from reoccurring in future, a geographical boundary was drawn up to determine the nature of the new territories created

in the former Louisiana and entering the Union. From then on, slavery was outlawed north of the 36°30' line of latitude, which corresponded to the southern border of Missouri.

This practice of admitting two states at a time remained in force for several decades. As such, the slaveholding Arkansas joined the Union in 1836, followed by the abolitionist Michigan the following year. Likewise, the entry of Florida, in the South, was counterbalanced by the entry of Iowa, which was a free state.

The Missouri Compromise was a major event in the history of slavery in the United States. The debate opened up by the membership of this new state allowed Americans to realise the importance of the question for the smooth running of the county and led politicians to reflect on the situation. However, the compromise proposed by Clay and signed into law by Monroe only offered a temporary solution to the problem and did not bridge the profound differences between the North and South. The treaty remained in effect for a little over 20 years before being replaced by the Kansas-Nebraska Act, which allowed inhabitants of the states to decide for themselves whether they wanted to practice slavery or not, in 1854. The division between abolitionists and slaveholders ultimately led to the American Civil War.

## THE MONROE DOCTRINE

It was not easy for a young nation like the USA to carve out a place for itself in the world order. It was even more difficult to make the European colonial powers, which dominated the world at that time, accept the country's newly acquired freedom. It was not until after two wars and half a century that Great Britain fully abandoned its American ambitions. After the Louisiana Purchase and the definitive withdrawal of the British, the acquisition of Florida from Spain allowed the American territory to be freed from its last European enclave.

In South America, several countries were also waging wars of independence in order to free themselves from Spanish domination. The USA supported this revolutionary impetus, although it still doubted whether this would permit the establishment of American-style democracies. The USA was the first colony to have gained independence, and planned to set itself up as a model and a guide for its younger South American relatives. However, the USA feared that Spain would refuse to let these new nations become independent and would retake them by force.

In this context, Monroe issued a statement on 2 December 1823 which became known as the Monroe Doctrine. However, this text was written not by the president himself, but by his Secretary of State, John Quincy Adams.

Portrait of John Quincy Adams, Secretary of State under Monroe and author of the Monroe Doctrine.

When Great Britain suggested a bilateral pact with the USA in order to defend themselves against France and Spain, the government was in favour of this. Monroe, who liked to surround himself with competent people and did not take decisions alone, nonetheless asked for the opinion of his right-hand man John Quincy Adams. Adams refused to enter into an alliance with a European power and decided to issue a unilateral declaration to serve as a warning to the colonising countries.

The Monroe Doctrine comprised three major principles:

- It developed the idea of non-colonisation, meaning that Europe had to refrain from creating new dependencies in the Western hemisphere.
- The USA proclaimed itself the protector of the revolutions in South America and encouraged driving European imperialism from the continent. This second point asserted the hegemony of the United States over all the Americas.
- In return, the United States would refrain from intervening in European matters.

In other words, the Monroe Doctrine stated that America belonged to Americans. Such a strong declaration could not fail to attract attention, and Americans were quick to react. Public opinion was divided: while some were unhappy that the statement threatened the peace and prosperity that had already been acquired, others praised the establishment of a solid basis for American foreign policy.

In any case, the leaders of the countries targeted by the statement seemed to hear its message loud and clear. In Europe, the Congress of Vienna (1814-1815) marked the end of Napoleonic imperialism and the major monarchies committed to supporting the absolute monarchy against any further revolutionary attempts. However, the European governments did not intervene in the revolutions in South America, led by men like Simón Bolívar (South American general and statesman, 1783-1830) and supported by the USA. Russia, which at that time occupied Alaska and coveted the Oregon region, also took heed of the warning. In 1821, the tsar extended the Russian border to the 51$^{st}$ parallel north, well to the south of Alaska, and halted the lucrative fur trade between Americans and Native Americans. After the doctrine had been issued, the Russians finally opted to abandon the Oregon region and withdrew towards Alaska.

The Monroe Doctrine is undeniably one of the highlights of Monroe's presidency, because it has been reused and interpreted up until the present day and even now serves as the basis for US foreign policy. Furthermore, this declaration allowed the country to define the place it wanted to occupy in the world order and above all on the American continent.

# IMPACT

Monroe's two terms as president are more complicated than they may seem at first glance, and summarise the major problems of the first decades of the history of the USA. Although Monroe has remained in the shadow of his illustrious predecessors, George Washington and Thomas Jefferson, his presidency is nonetheless of considerable interest and left a substantial mark on later American politics.

## THE BIRTH OF A GIANT

The USA came out stronger overall after Monroe's eight-year presidency: the country was bigger thanks to the acquisition of Florida and part of Texas, and had organised the new arrivals into free or slave states. Monroe's presidency also allowed the European colonial powers to be definitively driven from American territory and the sovereignty of the country to be protected.

The president and those around him also managed to give new momentum to American foreign policy by establishing a strong doctrine. Although this doctrine had no validity in international law, it marked the beginning of US hegemony on the American continent and the end of European interference in the country's affairs.

This doctrine has been taken up and reinterpreted by several American presidents over the years. In the 1840s, it was notably reused by President James K. Polk (1795-1849), who incorporated into his Manifest Destiny ideology, according to which the American nation had a divine mission to spread democracy and civilisation to the west. This new interpretation gave the doctrine a prophetic meaning. In 1904, Theodore Roosevelt added the Roosevelt Corollary, which asserted the USA's right to intervene militarily in the case of "Chronic wrongdoing, or an impotence which results in a general loosening of the ties of civilized society" in one of the countries in South America. This addition put an end to the inherent neutrality of the Monroe Doctrine and legitimised the USA's desire to expand, in particular towards Cuba and Panama. In 1962, John F. Kennedy cited the Monroe Doctrine to justify his action against Soviet missiles placed on Cuban territory.

The Monroe Doctrine has therefore evolved until the present day, but it is still the foundation of US foreign policy and justifies in particular the USA's power to interfere in the rest of the continent.

## FEET OF CLAY

In spite of everything, the growing power of the country was weakened by the tensions surrounding the issue of slavery. The situation of the black and Native American populations was a stain on this country, which set itself up as a model and a defender of democracy. In spite of a period of political calm during the Era of Good Feelings, Monroe proved unable to resolve this problem and his Missouri Compromise only put off the issue. Indeed, although the compromise was enough to calm spirits for a generation, it did nothing to erase the differences between the North and the South. Four decades later, the two sides embarked on an ideological war (the American Civil War), which ended with the abolition of slavery.

After Monroe's presidency, unity came to an end and the Era of Good Feelings turned into an era of bad feelings. In addition to the tensions between the abolitionist North and the slaveholding South, the Democratic-Republican Party split in 1824 over the choice of a presidential candidate. Supporters of John Quincy Adams, the former Secretary of State under Monroe, proclaimed themselves Republicans, while those in favour of Andrew Jackson founded the Democratic Party. Jackson was defeated by Adams in 1824, before being elected in 1828.

# SUMMARY

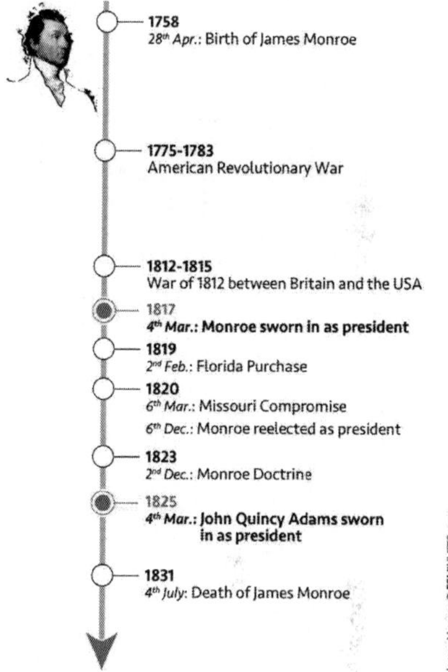

**1758**
28th Apr.: Birth of James Monroe

**1775-1783**
American Revolutionary War

**1812-1815**
War of 1812 between Britain and the USA

1817
**4th Mar.: Monroe sworn in as president**

**1819**
2nd Feb.: Florida Purchase

**1820**
6th Mar.: Missouri Compromise

6th Dec.: Monroe reelected as president

**1823**
2nd Dec.: Monroe Doctrine

1825
**4th Mar.: John Quincy Adams sworn
in as president**

**1831**
4th July: Death of James Monroe



- James Monroe was the fifth President of the United States of America. He occupied the White House between 1817 and 1825.
- Monroe was above all an excellent diplomat who worked

in France and Britain. He played an active part in the negotiations which led to the purchase of French Louisiana from Napoleon Bonaparte in 1803.

- Along with this predecessors Thomas Jefferson and James Madison, Monroe was one of the major figures of the Democratic-Republican Party, which split in 1824.
- His presidency has been described as the Era of Good Feelings due to the relative political unity of the period. However, this consensus was fragile and did not continue after the end of Monroe's second term.
- The USA bought Florida from Spain in 1819 thanks to the intervention of the commander of its armies, General Andrew Jackson, who pursued fugitive slaves and belligerent Native American tribes as far as Florida, before capturing several Spanish forts.
- The Missouri Compromise of 1820 regulated whether new states were free or slave states and calmed tensions between the North and South for a generation. However, it only delayed the need for a real solution, which would be found with the abolition of slavery at the end of the American Civil War.
- Monroe influenced the history of the USA by giving a new impetus to its foreign policy and finding a place for it in the world order, in particular thanks to the Monroe Doctrine. This doctrine, which even today underlies American foreign policy, forbade all European intervention in American affairs and vice versa. It was widely taken up and reinterpreted by subsequent presidents.

*We want to hear from you!*
*Leave a comment on your online library*
*and share your favourite books on social media!*

# FIND OUT MORE

## BIBLIOGRAPHY


- Cresson, W. (1946) *James Monroe*. Chapel Hill: University of North Carolina Press.
- Delacampagne, C. (2002) *Histoire de esclavage. De l'antiquité à nos jours*. Paris: Le livre de poche.
- Forbes, R. (2007) *The Missouri Compromise and its Aftermath*. Chapel Hill: University of North Carolina Press.
- Miller Center (No date) *James Monroe (1758-1831)*. [Online]. [Accessed 27 February 2017]. Available from: <http://millercenter.org/president/monroe>
- Schoell, F. (1965) James Monroe. *Histoire des États-Unis*. Paris: Payot. pp. 149-153.
- The American Presidency Project (No date) *Theodore Roosevelt, XXVI President of the United States: 1901-1909. Fourth Annual Message, December 6, 1904*. [Online]. [Accessed 27 February 2017]. Available from: <http://www.presidency.ucsb.edu/ws/?pid=29545>
- Thompson, P. (2000) *Cassell's Dictionary of Modern American History*. London: Orion.
- White House (No date) *James Monroe*. [Online]. [Accessed 27 February 2017]. Available from: <https://www.whitehouse.gov/1600/presidents/jamesmonroe>


## ADDITIONAL SOURCES


- Ammon, H. (1990) *The Quest for National Identity*. Charlottesville: University of Virginia Press.

- Cunningham, N. (1996) *The Presidency of James Monroe.* Lawrence: University of Kansas Press.
- Perkins, D. (1933) *The Monroe Doctrine, 1826-1827.* Baltimore: John Hopkins University Press.
- Sexton, J. (2012) *The Monroe Doctrine: Empire and Nation in Nineteenth-Century America.* New York: Hill and Wang.
- Unger, H.G. (2010) *The Last Founding Father: James Monroe and a Nation's Call to Greatness.* Philadelphia: Da Capo Press.

## ICONOGRAPHIC SOURCES

- Portrait of James Monroe. Royalty-free reproduction picture.
- Portrait of Elizabeth Monroe. Royalty-free reproduction picture.
- *Washington and Lafayette at Valley Forge*, painting by John Ward Dunsmore. Royalty-free reproduction picture.
- American Marines search for Native Americans during the Seminole War. Royalty-free reproduction picture.
- Portrait of John Quincy Adams, Secretary of State under Monroe and author of the Monroe Doctrine. Royalty-free reproduction picture.

## FILMS AND DOCUMENTARIES

- *The Monroe Doctrine.* (1939) [Short film]. Crane Wilbur. Dir. USA: Warner Bros.
- *The American President.* (2000) [Documentary]. Caroline

Waterlow. Dir. USA: PBS.

www.50minutes.com

Ebook EAN: 9782806290236

Paperback EAN: 9782806294265

Legal Deposit: D/2017/12603/99

Cover: © Primento

Digital conception by Primento, the digital partner of publishers.

Made in the USA
Monee, IL
07 July 2026